DE 0955 359708 9003

Dun Laoghaire-Rathdown Libraries
DALKEY LIBRARY
Inv/07 : L115   Price   E13.00
Title: Map of everything
Class: 821. FIT

KU-676-125

BAINTE DEN STOC

WITHDRAWN FROM
DÚN LAOGHAIRE-RATHDOWN COUNTY
LIBRARY STOCK

By the same author

Poetry
Swimming Lessons

As Editor
The Colour of The World
The Compass
Uncharted Voyage
Deep Canyons

ANNE FITZGERALD

The Map of Everything

BAINTE DEN STOC

WITHDRAWN FROM
DÚN LAOGHAIRE-RATHDOWN COUNTY
LIBRARY STOCK

First published in 2006
by Forty Foot Press
Box 10715, Glenageary, Co. Dublin, Ireland

Cover Design and Layout by A.J. Gatsby
Set in 10/16 pt Baskerville

Printed in Ireland by Wicklow Press Ltd,
The Murrough, Co. Wicklow

All rights reserved
© Anne Fitzgerald, 2006

The right of Anne Fitzgerald to be identified as author
of this work has been asserted in accordance with Section 77
of the Copyright, Designs and Patents Act 1988

*This book is sold subject to the condition that it shall not,
by way of trade or otherwise, be lent, resold, hired out
or otherwise circulated without the publisher's prior consent
in any form of binding or cover other than that in which it
is published and without a similar condition including
this condition being imposed on the subsequent purchaser*

A CIP record for this book
is available from the British Library
ISBN-0-9553597-0-8
978-0-9553597-0-5

To Sacha,
Duchess of Abercorn

Acknowledgements

Acknowledgements are due to the editors of the followings publications
in which some of these poems or earlier versions of them have appeared:

*The Black Mountain Review, Burning Bush, Foilsiú, Fortnight, Free Verse,
Kaleidoscope, New Welsh Review, Plains Song Review, Pushkin Journal,
The Recorder, Ropes, St. Andrew's College Celebrity Doodle Ugandan Project,
The Stinging Fly, Stand Magazine, Thornfield Anthology and Warp & Weft.*

Radio Broadcasts include: RTÉ Radio One and NPR Billings, Montana.

I should also like to thank Abraxas, Shane Harrison, Hilda Quin,
Thornfield Poets, Turoe Studios, and Kevin Whelan.

Contents

The Map of Everything

'No surface can be seen exactly as it is,
if the eye that sees it is not
equally remote from all its edges.'

Leonardo da Vinci — Notebooks Vol., 1:91

The Map of Everything

for Mike

Right from the start a little satchel is placed on the small of your back
carrying the weight of knowledge between your fine shoulder blades.

The world is folded in coloured pages, cut from equatorial rain
forests. A leg of lamb and a boot bound 'n numbered in a Collin's edition.

From mother's baking drawer you nick a sheet of grease-proof
usually kept to house the rising of her baking Alaska's. Down

on your hands and knees, you run a lead pencil over borders,
finger purple mountain ranges, tan river beds and yellow meadows,

mark cities out with red dots as if paintings bought. Window
-peeking through slits 'n ovals, you see silks sail straits to bellow

oceanic trade winds. Nutmeg and peppercorn fill cargo-holds.
Mint tea is served with roasted almonds before the scent of musk

controls the thrust of movement beneath the Bedouin flow
as the shape of the Ottoman Empire shifts under your hands;

tracing the Byzantium Empire from: Istanbul, Greece and the Balkans,
across Asia Minor, Egypt, and North Africa, and onwards towards Spain.

And like Suleiman the Magnificent you walk over mosaics and towns,
ride aqueducts as if merry-go-rounds to touch livelihoods hoodwinked

by traders as fluently as speech drifts past frescoes in Christian monasteries,
where castles on hilltops are lighthouses running light over battlefields

in the wake of action. You colour the rivers blue or try to, for a touch of crimson
seeps through the Nile, the Volga and the Danube as if the consecration, do this in

memory of me bit. You see Christendom under threat. Triangular flags at half-mast
stake new territory like learning by rote. Twelve twelve's are one hundred and forty

four. It is like flicking through an Encyclopaedia Britannica; you are catapulted by
the repetition of history's geography, as if watching distant houses burn in snow.

Latitude

I have seen in your eyes an inner light
that takes me towards that place of longing.
Somewhere beyond the horizon I enquire
as to the precise co-ordinates of these sea
grass fields where nymphs lull about in hulls:
mermaids comb their spirals beneath the sun.

In the same way you can quench the sun
from dog-days to leave an odd eclipse of light
trapped in starfish, guiding a forest of hulls
home to Atlantis; seahorses carry our longing
starboard, on course for deeper fathoms, below sea
-level we speak in an Aristotelian tongue, enquire

without conch or a knowledge of Greek, enquire
as to whether angels come from the sun
of man made things or riddles by sea
-faring merchants, voyaging to new found light.
For Velasquez and the like stirred a longing
in wanderlust: men bend the ribs of hulls

around the horn of capes, lost hulls
floored in myth, set oceanographers off to enquire
as to their whereabouts with sextant and longing.
Might dead-sea scrolls be read in the sun
or water cover the pattern of land in daylight,
might Noah's Ark be hoisted to ride the sea?

If you raise the sash on weightless sea
-side towns: ice cream windows and upturned hulls
by a boatshed or hoofed moons cobbling twilight
strands, ebb and flow of equinox tides enquire
after white horses running amok off sun
drenched hotspots, daiquiris by a pool stand longing.

And closing time brings no closure to this longing
save those who find their way below the silk of seas.
There monastral blues bath in a darker sun
fading deck chair stripes put out on other hulls
where divers find no shadows pass by or enquire
about the comings and goings of such light.

And in such light there rises a longing
for your sun-dark way with azure: sky to sea
edge-two-edge, little hulls push off to enquire.

Lexicon Tree

You peal the very bark of speech back
run your palms along language knots

finger hulls who will sail your sentenced seas
where from a crow's nest, land is shouted:

in the glint of movement a coded light talks back
as you imagine what da Gama might have seen.

You are bow and mast and sail, propelling me out
over your taught branches to stretch my present-perfect

under your yellow side of ripeness my words are wind
falls, conjugating tense shades of imperfect sweetness

beneath your voice a stammer sunders syllables.
Alexandra traces the shoreline of your narrative.

Chiaroscuro's Framing Technique

You hold out an arm like a Venetian arch
to touch the very fabric of thought
water pathways with no pavement cracks.

Squeezing imaginary tubes shapes your idea
of colour. Heavy reds spread: ivy on pebble dash.
Pigment pinking some previous façade of shades.

After your knowledge-pallet has mixed a blend
of primary light inward, towards a secondary dark
jade polar spots appear to chase shadow streaks.

A grace of creases fall from your velvet sleeve
blue-silk lined like a costume of sails billowing
in the Adriatic, faraway close to the foreground.

Dry mounted, hung from a let-on dado rail
in another world. Seen and not heard
your finishing touches lie in figures of speech.

Into the Square of Dawning

Your phrases could be hieroglyphics, scrawled shapes
articulating creations end in a radish sun-burst flourish

cut sound water-white. You chisel consonants into vowels
making a chiseller of love, rays fall as a kid-glove, gravel

under foot inclined to step-quick, inflects the arch of speech
in a natural gait reaching a larynx-stride like broken English

translates your copperplate curves between pale air-lines, each
parts blue sums of atmosphere, a translatable rhythm of breath

filling the darkness of some Egyptian tomb like a child-pharaoh
lies in waiting, hierarchy of needs triangulates splinters through.

Sweets

We'll say we make it up as we go along.
Once upon a time I swallow a pack of *love*
-hearts, digest raised words for later on.

Around the straight and narrow you peal
the very yarrow of my thoughts, neck
petals in a love-me loves-me not fashion.

The tissue of my dreams you open back
as a hard back waiting to be read;
mother-tongue of motion in invisible ink

in a straight backed chair you open purple
as a back and forth kind of thing,
the lavender in verbs, the lilac of speech.

I eat bulls eyes and see the black and white of it
as Snow White did, I blame Walt Disney,
Some day my prince will come, the notion of it

A Rough Sketch

Clematis trails your fresh washed gable end
beyond bracken and the purple of heather.

You hold the Cherry Orchard open and
in the shade of your shadow thyme nods-off:

about an August light, imaging squares and
snow or the oval of Fabergé in a Romanov's

pocket. I take a soft lead to your blank space
a good likeness darkens white, save the eyes

hard to get just so, as clearing in a forest
where mushrooms might look up to bark.

If the pupil needs a touch of cinnamon
then for the iris say a dash of lamp-black.

Light loses face, finds a pleasure in petals
opening out in the deeper frame of things.

Clear Vision

I saw the lightning
in your head
kindle what is past,

take root like wildfire,
redden nowness,
as if a cigarette lit in

the globe of my palm
after rain,
and sulphur inhale

the dampness
of our
yellow distances.

Speech

An early moon
pale as snowdrifts
traces your ability
to go through
the motions,
as you
wax and wane;

you insinuate
a noun into a verb
as if a path
of light making
its way across
early shadows

snow creates
in its blindness,
to cover your
visionary vowels
falling round
and slender
from the oval
of your mouth.

Letting Go

Neither an instamatic flash nor the fan-fair
of make believe can contain it, save a blue paused belief
punctuating conversational slip stitches,
embroiders speech in the ochre of bridges;
a suspension of longing arcs your Godlike narrative head
-on, unravels the indigo of what's not said,
threads olive in vain through my chambers' inner Jericho
as if plovers are being released from a high up window.

REM GMT

From a restlessness that comes midway
through night, revisiting in broad daylight
to pull your small hours inside out.

If you could un-dream: orange sets the sun (as jelly
on a plate), curved round, slips into waves (wibbly
-wobbly wonder of it all, aqua miniatures a keepsake)
just as a thrupenny bit in a mission box darkens by
its fall, reaching Equatorial rain forests so lush
with Cistercian cowls and trees bleeding rubber.

For should the quality of rain droppeth as religiosity
drip-dropping from your God above. Clouds burst
rainbows flourish, yet the gold-pot is an unsaid rosary
its recovery a novena not heard at first. Yes, an upside
down bucket doubles for a ding-dong announcing
a benediction of sound towards Glenstal Abbey.

Down Main Street ding-a-ling of H.A. Cole's pharmacy
hinges darkness back like evenings' cock-stretch.
Elements and minerals glass shelf lined, oceanic earth
sporting its logarithmic pigments as a Velspar chart:
sulphurs' marigold, violet iodine, never mind young piggy
in d'middle, gardenia blossoming phosphorus blanc.

Beside the chemist shop Gasparro's all purpose grocery
store bright as the black hole of Calcutta, an unsold forest
of newspapers scaffold your yard of makeshift counter: ply
-wood rich with pink lucky bags, Peggy's Legs and penny
-dreadfuls'jaw breaking a generation of little milk teeth.
From S-hooks Fyffe's are hanging shadows into jungle dark

yellowing green, prayer-winds ripen like the spread of word
world wide, pupated vision watches its own demise self-made
to tunnel wormwood. Conditions are favourable for the spread
of potato blight are they not, not at all, quite the reverse in fact.
From here to there sleepless toss-turns wait for dawn to bring
on those dancing girls, those lovely sirens of daylight-night.

Trio

1. Given Up

At an abandoned railway line, sleepers rust,
forgotten, as the child of a one night stand.

2. After Rain

Eucalyptus drowns air, silver odour of bark,
scythe leaves cut spearmint cobbles for nostrils,
in, out, to the very shape of breath itself.

3. Thinking Flags

It seems as though its all about light
about its orange giving and navy receiving
its plum suppression and orchard's refraction
that ricochets the heart's very soul of thought.

New Year's Eve Skinny Dip

In memory of Dorothy Molloy

On Dalkey Hill little lights come on, as if a Dorothy Cross Ghost ship,
its granite Quarry's rock-face winks in glints. Your dying sun pinks windows
clean as flesh fingers ripples walking out to sea, drawn by the lightship you were.

Midway across the Atlantic, midshipmen spot the horizon arising to bend
light, light years away. Year in, year out, anchors drop. Ropes are thrown
across decks, and all triangular sails are hoisted to the god of a new world.

For you have looked upon the shape of stars, seen dark spots tip-toe lunar craters,
harnessed the Jovian satellites in pursuit of longitude and its latitudinal swings.
You have seen the origin of distance. You have measured the heavens as they open —

Middle Distance Abridged

Ever before we meet foundations are laid
all summer long as bulbs about to flower.
From the forest floor climbers start out
growing up to bend a later light, where
dogwood bright as Brighton rock strays
between weather and your open gate.

Sultans might thread past this gate
to fold and unfold silk, vermilion laid
out to tailor Europe or weigh stray
peppercorns. Spice and rumours flower
an appetite for your turmeric touch, where
the sound of wing beats open out

Hazel, too cold to give fragrance out.
Flagstones usher empires through gate
states, altering marks of mappery where
distance widens then shrinks, discovery laid
bare. Before time even gardenia can flower
if taken in. Blossoms thrust and stray —

Crusaders half expected beliefs will stray
as medieval saints. Charters and seals carryout
measurements, but what's not drafted will flower
from seeds to be sown beyond HighGate.
Slips will be passed on. Roads laid
down and bypassed to an elsewhere.

If you believe in angels somewhere
before all of this a feather might stray.
Magellan comes full-circle, quest laid
to rest. Icebergs melt, how things turn out
remains to be seen. I unhinge your gate:
an amethyst boarder, Aurora Borealis in flower.

You tease roots anxious for next year's flower
to show its true colour. Signs where
more eyes hide from behind this gate.
Somehow a plumb-line of chance goes astray
creating new regions. Purple Hearts given out.
Rain lingers on fuchsia bells, lightly laid.

Laid back in time poppies can flower
beside your gate: swings across to where
a stronger light strays, spreads wildfire out.

Double Exposure

And in the whites of your eyes Alaska drifts —
past rhododendrons and the promise of summer.
The pop of ladyfingers plucked from foxgloves
velvet removes of you, lying beyond a gate
where you sit with a teacup and sun on your face
under a New England shade of weather forecasts.

Light rain still scents that time we cut flowers
as a photo grafts a hold on the moment
its dry lining folds our sky away below sea level.

Down by an oyster bed we square a roundness
of our peril, scattering airs and graces of stars.
Over sea-grass fields lapwings are snowdrops
whilst daffodil sails draw the mauve of evening
to port, in a scheme of things laid up in lavender.

The Royal Marine

Mock pillars frame my walkway to a lost splendour
cornices and Polyfilla collide, bay windows look out
past an artillery of masts in Bligh's Asylum Harbour
where the Mail Boat still berths the right to travel

and I think of you gliding over marble squares to sign
Smyth, never slip Y for an I over a watermark crown.
Upon off white, ink dries out our name between faint blue

lines like an upturned hull sun bathing on a slipway
whose barnacles cling to stay as children given up.
Lobsters chase red shadows around orange pots of sun,
anchors bear the erosion of salt voyages.

Whistler's ships and flying fish are Stations of the Cross
in a room where women wait for men, as I for you.
A baby grand plays a slow air from the turn of the century.

Vanishing Point

Tell me again how it was, could it have been just so
sun on a trade wind and a breeze coming off the sea?

Between the dashes and dots two miles as the crow flies
frogmen dive through diesel spots, ripple rainbows —

Periwinkle blue and silver mackerel arc out little circles.
The V of hulls cut waves as diviner's hazel looking for water.

Beyond driftwood fishermen cast nets, under catgut diamonds
succulent flesh dries out, scales bask along planks to half-make

salt-moon impressions, like the clip clop of hooves on a strand
run over by the wash. Pearl shells catch light after Bell Rock,

invisible strokes come out of the blue, push and pull goes on.
Tripods are easels set up for the unknown to become known.

Material Stretcher

You're such a dab hand
at swinging the lead.
Were you not supposed

to be nailing gold studs
into plaited braid? Instead
you run your hands

the length of my body,
touch crevices bound
for overlap.

You tuck chestnut horsehair
carefully out of sight.
In the hem you finger

an oceanic darkness
where man's shadow
once trod;

perfumes a seabed
of drowned decks,
instruments fathoms

unmeasured, to pattern
a remnant's watermark.
Ship to shore foghorn

hides till springs show
circles, circling inner
rounds of themselves in you.

Equinox Post Mortem

Honestly there is no doubt, you get
away with bloody-blue murder.
With each intake of breath you run

circles around all in sundry
as if making a Havana work
alcoves of a room.

I would have kept heaven open
after hours, prodded the sun
for extra shine, let dawn stay out

to skinny dip with an apricot moon
till the first train pulls out. You see
whistles blow at level crossings:

stations flit by, children wave from beaches,
marram grass holds sand and the sea at bay.
To be honest, I would have pulled in the tide.

American Snap Shots

Now what with your bottom half lifted sash-high, past
cacti shoots, lets WKNY play over heads of hopscotch kids,
chalking one through ten on their sidewalk squares.

Every now and then voices feel the redder
self of heat, reddest just before bed
like drops wheeling water into wine.

Sunburnt leatherette sees you put the backs
of your hands under your knees on account
of shorts, far too short believe you me.

What of the way your Chrysler Bluebird slows
to a stop, having turned right on red, its tail lights
dissolves distance into suburbs beyond Diamond Row.

In your rear view mirror: at the corner of Seventh
and Eight, Ninth's long shadow over shadows children
bathing in the burst water hydrant, sprays their skin

all over, as if the pollen stain of stamen; dries off
in a sun that's been around the block, brings water beads
to its knees, towards a circular movement of prayer.

Blue rinse brigades soldier on to light Orange Lane
with Zimmer frames. A convention of arched shoulders
in parking lots, wait like kids in a school line,

for brogue-less nannies to pick them up.
Hershey Bars and fat free buns weigh trunks down:
Key Lime pie and blue crab-cakes take corner wide,

as you tuck into Pepperidge Farm's *Orlando's*,
trailing crumbs along interior stitching,
as if a line of coke you once had.

At St. Sebastian's, incense draws you in,
to light candles at St. Anthony's feet
as he holds a child on an open book.

A garbage truck pulls up, an ice-cream van
jingles after dark, gives out raspberry ripple
with a dash of lime, like tubs sold at the Gaiety,

when Maureen Potter was pantomime.
Woodbines and *Sweet Afton's* sold
as singles in the aisles, from a fruit box

hung ribbon-deep, off pretty young
things with Broadway eyes,
when safety curtains kissed the stage.

On the home stretch, past Radio City,
the Russian Tea rooms and FDR Drive
you turn the radio on to drown the city.

Three Lovely Lassies from Bannion say
their going back to, *the Black Hills of Dakota*,
to say nothing of *Blue Birds over the White*

Cliffs of Dover, moored as fog over Mid-Town,
while Queen Elizabeth sails up the Hudson;
flags fly, knots turn miles, geographies collide.

Welcome to Seligman Birthplace
of Historic Route 66

'And the gates of it shall not be shut at all by day: for there shall be no night there'.
Revelation Ch.21:25

Driving through the Painted Desert your left arm turns pink, steering the car your
raspberry thumb rests on the wheel as if a summer fruit; holds the avocado road
straight ahead of nut brown distant streaks, shadowing mandarin till vermilion
creeps like a thief in the dead of scarlet, shows blueberry up; gooseberry flecked
as the night his hand left your face. In the wing mirror broken capillaries look
you in the eye as plain as day, or the Plains stretched in front of your windshield.

Driving past the Hover Dam, head west, then due south for Flamingo Road.
A mosaic arises like a mirage thrown together, a bit out of kilter: a Pyramid,
an Eiffel Tower, Liberty, and a Sphinx appear as if a Nevada-Disney
for grown-ups; Our century's Mecca where ancient and modern worlds collide.
Would Henry the Eight's Thomas Moore approve of this Western Utopia
where Protestant, Catholic and Jew flock? Where green-backs are the currency

of inclusion and the ability to count is like a credo of the day, day in day out.
Forty-five degrees north, and twelve point two degrees west is where Venice
is, on the Atlas. It's as if awoken from their slumber, Michangelo 'n Leonardo do
a nixer, they make something out of nothing, transporting to Nevada; Venice.
Half the length of O'Connell Street this version is, as spied through Galileo's O,
though not a sign of his four moons of Jupiter nor young Cosimo de' Medici.

On the second floor of this hotel a Grand Canal flows above croupiers, as if the Arno
is in sight. Gondolas bob and nod under the Bridge of Sighs, past Armani 'n Gucci.
The smell of opulence perfumes every nook and cranny of this let-on palatial Uffizi.
Coming in from one hundred and twenty degrees, to air that goose-pimples skin,
rising as if cacti in the distance of angel-hair spaghetti. Look up and up to Botticelli's
octagonal dome beyond flying buttress, stood on marble, you thinking it's the Dumo.

Fresh air courses the Venetian's circulatory system. No heat of day nor sun comes in.
Neon lights herald brightness like Lucky Strikes burning holes in the darkness *...to
lead us into temptation...* to *put another nickel in the nickelodeon...to give us our daily
bread...* in this amusement arcade, so that we *...will be done on earth as it is in heaven...*
to... *deliver us from evil...*slots and wheels and chips*...for the kingdom and the glory...*
of brimstone burning brightly and a single flame flickering as if a christening tongue.

Handcuffed to a one arm bandit like a naked mannequin in Sack's shop front,
you chew a stick of Hollywood gum as Arkle had a blade of grass; knock back
Long Island Iced Teas as if lemonade drank after sunny spells in Adam's yard.
You'll pull the arm from its socket, develop tennis elbow as quarters will feed
your hunger to win, waiting for three fruit to fall in line: plumbs, pears or apples.
For Newton's windfall to free you from a south facing pebble-dashed, semi-D,

to hear a ding ding-a-ling-ling, as if Niagara's Horseshoe Falls spill, ding-a-lang.
Here tell, did that here one travel through those them time zones to sit at this there
machine? A beauty ain't she. She be the one that will bring forth your future in
president's heads, quarters my friend, quarters I say, not army nor segmented kind;
better than await the fall of lady-luck's dice at black jack, poker or her roulette spin
...*All you need's a strong heart and a nerve of steel...Viva las vegas, viva las vegas...*

The eye in the sky keeps vigil. Even clubs watch spades and kings queens, while dice
study baize as big bucks are shelled out for broken dreams like the shards of marriage
delft lying on living room floors...*remember that I had a swingin' time, viva las vegas...*
Look. Over there is Caesar's Place. Different but the same as the one on Bray seafront;
above its promenade of baby-blue chipped railing-paint. The sea whitewashes sound,
darkens shapes to light, shifts grains in the algebra of surf and the calculus of currents.

The Island

And what of the day we went to the island
when the sun was out of its mind, sky-high
with rain dried clouds hung out to whiten
like the White Sands of New Mexico.

There you are Laurence of Arabia, on top
of dunes, at sea in this desert of gypsum:
(add rain to create a plaster of Paris ocean).
I am an extra in an old black and white,
staring into its glare for *The Lone Ranger*
to take me in to the distance with its credits.

A breeze brings me back to our circle of land
moored in front of The Vico, yet miles to Sorrento.
Cayenne heat and the bee hived huts of the Pueblo
face us, in the harbour, *Santa Fe* bobs with other hulls.
Sea once covered State said a Los Almos Times head
-line, before Columbus, before Hiroshima or Chernobyl.

Our tumble (sea) weed, catches outboard motors
between waves and goose pimples on sea spray.
The sun leans in to evening, kissing ripples,
lipstick smears lapis lazuli: a set blush on blue.

Games

Adjusting the clothesline for a net, we play Wimbledon out the back.
Rita climbs a make-shift ladder, places a Bentwood from our kitchen
on Gleason's party wall, takes her umpire's chair, as cool as a breeze
and shouts, *Out. Advantage, Borg.* You can not be serious, I yell, again

and again. From her bird's eye she spies through Fogarty's palm
planted in Eighteen Forty by Captain Bligh's light-footed men
when they came to build John Rennie's Pier at Kingstown.
Granite hewn from Dalkey Quarry, carried by the Atmospheric Railway.

One penny a day is what Great Uncle Jack hears men got before he takes
the Kings Shilling, legs it with his mother's gas meter money,
joins the British Navy, sails the seven seas with Veronique tattooed
to his right bicep. She hails from the Golden Vale. In Martinique of a Friday

they met. Jack writes home, slips a snapshot by Chambers of Lands End
into his onion aerogram; like skin their wrapped around each other,
behind them the lighthouse shoot up as if a baptismal candle, annunciates
the advent of their days under the eye of Gustaves's Liberty.

He tells how he worked a bar off-Broadway back in Forty-Five,
great money to be made, till he runs off when a guy pulls a Magnum
on July Fourth, independence declares his swayed *Wild Turkey* shots
heard across Duffy and Time Squares where Citizen Kane fills screens

beside cowboy Reagan's giddy-ups, down dirt tracks... *on the trail
of the lonesome pine*...making for the big house on Pennsylvania Avenue.
Reruns of Laurel 'n Hardy air as wasp's bee-line Robinson's Barley
Water, muslin covered on Rita's lawn lies still. *New Balls Please,*

she roars, as evening turns in on itself, echoes little revolutions
across William's asphodels, yellowing amber dusk. Lights come on
on Dalkey Hill as if an advent calendar opening up. *Game, Set and Match.*
A net jump and a handshake; behind a rebellion of shadow implodes.

A Fruitless Passion

At Bullock a female bachelor boards
our bus. She blows gin 'n tonic kisses,
fogs the glass as though a lovers cheek
who might gather this show of affection
as if red roses thrown upon a stage.

Between Jack's Cross and Hollow Pass
she runs her palms over a lemon's yellow body,
cuts a half-moon (with her pocket Swiss
knife) lets its flesh slip into her mouth as if holy
communion or another's tongue 'n cheek.

At noon she takes away the sins of the world
and the lamb of God as she beats her fist lightly
to her breast. Angelus bells ring sound round.
She dreams of Gordon's and Schweppes,
the clink-clank of cubes, the sharpness of rind

in narrow slim-Jim's; and missed benefits-in-kind.
By her feet a dozen oranges rest in a string bag
criss-crossing skin, to make diamonds of peel,
ambers her dream's hulls as if pinks moored
at sunset, pelicans fly, water laps Longboat Quay,

across the street from where she shook
the life from a tangerine tree. You see, she
has a thing for fruit, of the citrus variety;
of how they might enhance a drink, think
of Pimm's No.1 or a virgin Bloody Mary.

Every year she makes this pilgrimage, prays
to the God of cocktail umbrellas and celery
sticks, all the while saying St. Jude's prayer;
for a woman to help study her hydrangeas
and a man to prune her box hedge right back.

First Watch

It was there in Glove Market that I eyed you finger
-ing the inner silk of pink-kid, calf-tan and ivory black
lined up as if a light inventory marching down Glass

Row, tip-toeing cobbled puddles after rain
distorts interiors: knifes 'n forks on kitchen
tables not quite centred, portraits hang askew

as a breeze makes its way over saddles
rearranges family albums and the power
of saints. Local legends and foreign myths

will matter not, empty places will be set
vigils will be lit. You run your index
around oilcloth squares, make memory

cards of your tablecloth, play X's and O's
for a roll call hindsight did not foresee; the right
light-fingered touch that took your left eye out.

Northern Latitudes

You spread thick strokes from your pallet knife
adding a topcoat to the Christmas cake,
cut a square of darkness rum has bound, it's like

the lava fields of Keflavík making for Reykjavík
to the interior, creation's alpha; a desert of rock
exists as a civilisation and a bas-relief of black
earth aerates aeons to pumice, weather-shapes.

Frost dusts moss as if sieved, in the back
-ground seafarers, Columcille and Vikings
appear and disappear from view like tourists.

Fingering almond paste, arsenic alive 'n kicking.
It takes candied peel and green Maraschinos for
you to peek at the Northern Lights. Look

-out, somewhere over Parliament Fields
towards the tectonic plates you will think
Mac Neice's shadow waves. Snow stiffens
like Royal icing, beyond glaciers and poetics.

Baptismal Under Painting

In that window of night, dawn drags itself through
an earlier light, day is threading across horizons
from Timbuktu to Galway Bay —
fish prepare for the spines of hulls, the casting of nets
and for shoals of men to reinvent themselves in the gutting.

Reading the Archives

Click of the polo ball rolls green in the Phoenix Park
hooves horseshoeing grass close noon after day.
Sycamores amber shade as the five lamps come on
and Bridie Gargan meets her maker at the hand
of a dickey-bowed petty thief. For Pilot View's
his sanctuary, or Shangri-La, tra-la-la, hiding out

in the attorney general's seaside haven of light, out
the Bullock Road. Fishermen strip hulls like the ark
before the flood, silvering a pier to scale the view
rotund, throw guts back, heads saved for dog-days.
Casting their lines towards bluebottle heat, hand
over fist. Hooks make their way beneath on

-coming waves, fleshing out blue from white on
account of pneumatic currents wheeling about.
Labradors paw bladder rack to catch the hand
-maiden's green sleeve: cuffs turned up, stark
as winged collars, goblets bone-dry as midday
catch a Venetian noon, gold-leafing a blown view.

Eastwards towards Scotsman's Bay to review
the Mirabeau. Here off-shore account holders on
expenses ordered cockles on a bed of avarice. As day
turns to night, asylum seekers lived at this site. Out
on Morecambe Bay cockle-pickers disappear. Larks
sound across shorelines as if immigration's hand

-break. Coast guards' binoculars watch the hand
of God at bay. Radar screens peruse the view
picking up a foreign movement in the dark.
Search and rescue crafts patrol white horses, on
and off. Shergar's ghost illuminates out
casts, brings them ashore to join day

trippers. For it is in the clarity of day
that our true reflection is seen, hand
-held, from glass tumblers of stout.
Deer run past the Arras into the view
of headlamps and headlines, somewhat on
-settling; *Minister and boy in the Park.*

And in Ryan's of ParkGate Street underhand
talk opens Sunday; different points of view
articulate the onslaught like a prophet cast out.

Loreto Abbey Convent School for Girls

to Anne Tuffy

...this seaside republic is shaping a little Machiavellian army...

Ten miles out from Eden Quay, on the No. Eight Bus, Sr. Francis
Teresa Ball's Tudor cruciform structure lies facing Maiden Rock.
Granite built in the Eighteen Forties; hewn from Dalkey Quarry.
At dawn a procession of habits bathe in Nun's Pool, prior to chalk
-ing blackboards, rubbing off daily knowledge and compulsory
roll calls. Boys from St. Michael's call us Virgins on the Rocks
a far cry from Leonardo's, hanging beside our Founder and Mary
Queen of Angels, d'Loreto motto, sewn to our blazer breast pocket.
Josephine O' Neill bursts out of her peacock gymslip, in a run
and pole vault jump over Sr. Helen's horse, at physical education.
Her white aertex splits as clouds, pregnant with rain, opens —

Eva Ringwood is putting basketballs back in the pavilion
having netted ball after basketball ball on the tournament court.
She's tipped for Head Girl, as her skirt is the right length above
the knee; Oh but to wear that badge over the right breast,
is to open doors to, the Civil Service or the Banking profession.
Eva is an A student who has a very hungry comprehension
for Maths, so much so that her teacher Mrs. Unger who, when
not attending to Mr. Unger's manly needs, is kind of half in love
with her. Mrs. U tells all to Father Martin in Friday's confession
after bouillabaisse and rye; made by nuns who bake communion
for priests to dole out at mass, before they count the collection.

Eva thinks Ms. Everlast could be *Jean Brodie*, with her Scottish
accent. She'd be in the habit of talking of sex without explanation
of what one ought to expect. Our green fingered Mr. Edward Lock
runs his pinkies through Sr. Basil's purple clematis which overlook
Sr. Camilla's broad bean plot marked out like an Ordnance Survey
map. Squares to round our perspective of where we inhabit, a British
Colombian Officer says on the second line of our geography book.
Everlast has us for ethics, extols her virtues of the artistic nature
of our souls *...soul of my saviour sanctify my needs...*, as one body
we sing, profess our faith around the grotto in an open air procession
for the Blessed Virgin, who looks like the bottle of Lourdes water

standing on Mother Columbus's workbench where Anne and Kevin
have an arrowhead puncture their wooden heart of make-believe;
yet they will have three children and a plastic Christ on the ash dash
-board of his father's XJS. Mornings spill through the glass passageway
to illustrate the Stations, his weight under wood and the betrayal of thorns.
How IHS shines like the miraculous medal hanging from Mary's neck
as she folds the corner of her white page back, makes a triangular peek
like Mont Blanc, who's cap peeps out of Mrs. Fennel's check pocket.
This is her instrument of war; black marks fall as if mountaineers climb
-ing slopes, joined-up writing scatters like casualties in homework books.
Her Chinese ink underlines and questions words in their making of sentences.

In the Concert Hall, *Snow* falls on deaf ears, as Sr. Jerome plays Elgar
on the grand piano proud as punch, showing-off its every movement.
Seated in the gallery, alto to the right, soprano on the left, we sway
with her metronome, find a melody to sing in harmony to; grace notes
fall between octaves as sunlight finds a blind spot above the mahogany
floorboards like smoke caught in light, or Sharon Kelly behind the bike
shed, with ten Marlboro in her paw and her mother's book of matches
from Dr. Zhiavigo's night club. Hauled over the coals in the Head's study.
Sr. Borgias draws Sharon out about how her Ma dances each night away
yet manages to put cheddar cheese on a slice of Brennan's batch for a pack
lunch; having scoured the bath with Ajax when she gets home. Mrs. Kelly's

smoke rises blue over breakfast like the stream of consciousness Sr. Borgias
runs in her head, or d'Vinci's, behind his virgin and child. Twice a week,
Lavinia O' Tool tells us to, *open all windows, breathe in, fresh air.* She'd split
the wind and atoms before the bell; jumping from shoots to logarithm tables
to her pet subject, the liver-fluke, a *hermaphrodite who has he and she bits.*
From the back row, *do you get that sort of thing in humans, Miss?* Fay Lynch
wants to know, we can't conceive this as we are still trying to get our heads
around the immaculate conception stuff and Albert's theory. Yet, relatively
speaking it was Michangelo's *David* has us in stitches, not Ms. Olive Firth's
still fruit life. Her HB pencils, poster paints and coloured threads from Cleary's
haberdashery sees us paint and embroider a fire screen tapestry of Dalkey church.
Down its aisle Nuala will be wheeled in six months time after a hit and run.

Jackson Browne's *Running on Empty* will be played. The why and what is
it all about, will raise its head prematurely, like a white lily before its time.
In the rose garden Sr. Assumpta collects fallen pink-apricot petals religiously
to make pot-pourri for the boarders dormitory, it's all the rage. Mr. Edward Lock
lets *Le Vie En Rose* slip out his mouth, lingers behind Sr. Octavo's rhododendron
bush as if a veil drawn at vespers. Kindling he'd collect for the refectory's
hearth to warm knees and damp spots. God but his *Old Spice* wouldn't half work
the corridors you'd think him the Queen of the surf, crashing rocks below
Convent lay-lines, in a whorl of a Guinness wave as Orff's Carmina Burana plays
tides. His scent ripples darkness like a backstitch in Sr. Gracie's sew

-ing. Her Singer's foot marches over gingham as he slips inside her bobbin
a drop of three-in-one. On Concepta Ryan's Walkman, Talking Heads play,
Once in a Lifetime, to daisy chains lying spent on the grass hockey pitch.
She halves and quarters half-time oranges, runs on with Mi-Wadi and Kimberly
Mikados at matches for the Loreto Shield; coveted by the nation's secondary
league, it stands on parquet flooring outside Miss Daphne Black's door.
Inside, Daphne waters asphodel's from the class of eighty-three, dabs a touch
of Four Seven Eleven on her wrists before taking out the Duraglit to polish
prefect badges, given to a handful, at two o'clock at the first Assembly of each
new year, to lead them into temptation in the spirit of *Maria Regina Angelorum;*
arrange their Debs Ball in Jury's Hotel and *The White Horse Inn,* drama society.

Of Borgias angels few will survive the eternal shame of that monstrous Rag Day.
Kerry will cut her wrists thrice at a bed-sit in Donnybrook; become a Moonie
and sell roses on the streets of Wyoming. Maureen will be a casino eye in the sky
in Vegas, having moved from Silicon Valley after implants. And as for Cherry,
will she go on to squeeze black-heads from wealthy chins and run a halfway
house for wayward girls, off the Fulham Palace Road, having heard The Clash
sing *London Calling,* at Saint Francis Xavier Hall in eighty-five? Ah yes, Verity
will give her baby up; spend years in and out of St. John of God's in search
of little Joy. For all her promise, after a brief sojourn behind a Harrods jewellery
counter, Eva heads for the Grand Canyon. She looks down the Bright Angel
Trail, re-imagines jack knife diving at Blackrock Baths, and lets fly —

through the centuries of rock; past corals and sea lilies in the creamy top layer
deposited by the Kaibab Sea, she thinks these Coconino Cliffs could be Dover
and of that French school tour, the rose window at Notre Dame, light splinter
-ing colour red as if cayenne limestone beyond Hermit shale, through glacial
shifts, to the sea of Cortés, back again to butte temples, thrones and rock towers.
At Vasey's Paradise red monkey flowers thrive as if flames, like the ones blown
out of proportion when Eva touched Ms. Everlast, *asserting her very own Adam*
she says; hides him till she fingers vermilion cliffs, ponderosa pines and cotton
-wood, freefalling in the Abyss, the sky has her under thumb, as if the ladybird trail
-ing Peach Road to Diamond Peak, where the Rio Grande flows into the Canyon
on her map. Out the class window, beyond granite walls she looks, towards Dalkey

Sound, hears the Mail Boat making for Dún Laoghaire. The Atmospheric Railway
Line carried granite, hewn from Dalkey Quarry for the building of Kingstown
Pier; into the mouth of its Harbour King George IV sailed. *Eva are you paying attention
or homage to Poseidon, what could be more captivating than the Navajo Falls?* Miss. Payne
asks in the last minutes of geography. *I feel like a Spanish adventurer in search of Seven
Cities of Gold, unable to find a route to the Colorado River; as it surges into House Rock
Rapids in Marble Canyon. Created to divide living worlds from the lands beyond death,
this place was. A geologic cross section reveals granite at its base and San Fran Peaks
in the distance. And at Lava Falls, marigolds shine as if a stack of Conquistador coins.
Piñon and juniper trees…,* we get the picture and the gist that you've listened, Miss. Payne
says, so you've been there? *Why no Miss, not yet that is, but who knows, one fine day…*

41

The Burden of Proof

You do a bit of spring-cleaning in the ochre of October
find cobwebs silvering light's corners, alive in the afterglow.
On a node's strand you weave invention into texture
seek foundation in setting-out colour. In due course bold
strokes brush paleness skin deep, purple-pinks-green-yellow.
Dots, tiny dots cluster, shape matters form, a cacophony
left to its own devices, impressionist in parts some say
to the point of cliché. In all manner of words you draw
perspective out to view blue vowels and consonants askew.

Under foot autumnal leaves crisp-crunch heading across hockey
pitch-black at five after four, sticks bully darkness echoing hollow
breaths, length of the all weather, and a white ball rounds speed
chalk marks ghost boundaries of who's off side, whistle out inside.
Into canvas runners shoe whitener is seeping deeper and deeper.
Above on the laundry pitch nuns washed linen, hung out to dry
left of wild roses like the expectation of sex; solid carbolic red —
knuckles knock a lather out, loosens flaxen threads to take away
our sins of this world, stray windfalls sweeten a walled orchard.

How the early hours ransack your mind, turning the blessed
virgin blue of order towards St. Anthony's dark-brown habit
of finding things, he accepts coins like nobody's business,
gives out no receipts, yet keeps such stuff that's gone astray:
odd socks, numbers on beer mats and intellectual property.
If floated on the NYSE, Anto. Inc., shall tot up the dividend
for how things might have been in terms of negative equality
spotting weakness in the bull to bear false witness against
what is not index linked. You've a somewhat aperitif quality

able to drink atmosphere in, giving it a pure swaying zest
in a room that's seen it all before we meet only twice weekly,
anticipation is the prelude, going through the motions
achieves nothing more or less than a heightened awareness.
From room service's a la cart we pick cheese; Black Diamond,
toothpicks sport triangular flags, appears to be flying buttress
arching our dome of intention, prayers reach a higher ground
find taking root hard to stomach the storm's eye, particularly
despite the fact that day in day out you have preyed and pray.
Soul of my saviour sanctify my needs… Along Convent Road

house-to-house enquiries; knock-knocking, tea and sympathy
is your foot in her door as you thread my anaglyptic hallway
just killing time as if your tastes for dialogue are vespers at hand.
Roasting conkers split; hard eye of needle threads twine through,
sits on a plump knot, knock-knock who's there, tongues flames.
Say if you'll turn over a new leaf, watch its delicate veins brown
and the old make little dolmens in the back garden of your mind
for the foot soldiers on the way who become casualties by light.
Sycamore catch the host-moon before dawn closes nights' day.
Into your brightness of shadows I commend this fiction unbound.

Sfumato Rosary

Come the middle of d'week you'd always start
an auld novena, what with a hail and holy Mary
mumbled under breath, as a copper kettle boils over
below on the Aga; a steam geyser in your kitchen,
barely making-out Orange Pekoe snug beside
Darjeeling, nor broken vanilla pods who pleasure

fine grain cane. Often you'd find a pleasure
in tearing corners off Manhattan Nuts, like start
-ing stamp collecting. From the off you're beside
yourself waiting for reverse charges beyond Mary
-ville, or it is two blocks south of Hell's Kitchen
where lines lengthen as days grow shorter over

Grand Central, tucked up in some hostel out over
42nd ? I keep the wolf from the door by pleasure
-ing others, send greenbacks back to a darkened kitchen
tick-tocking rations like a threat of rain, as if a false start.
From Herald, Union and Sheridan Squares I send Mary
cards, a triangle she makes, arching grotto-like beside

her telephone. Anyway this is all somewhat beside
the point for it takes more than a flight over
the transatlantic in a Tabasco haze of Bloody Mary's,
dashed with a plethora of Worcester, to find a pleasure
ground. Perhaps I might make good in fits and starts
to begin with, dance a half-set around the kitchen

dresser, still breaking habits are far harder than kitchen
-ware. Yes, Coney Island's quite like Bray, beside
the sea. My letters will say they gave me a start
Macy's did and chose to, imagine, pass me over
for your wone from Woodenbridge. Pleasure
was derived from this, can you believe it Mary?

Never mind, for I to have a touch of Mary
Magdalene and can kneel with d'best be kitchen
sinks: blue virginal folds unfolding family pleasures.
How candy floss sweetened our childhood pink beside
Bray Head; the cross on its crown is Christ over
Rio de Janeiro, cloudless skies crucified from the start.

By the Glory Be's start, Mary
wells up pleasure less prayers in a kitchen
-net, beside sights that lie turned over.

The Builder's Labourer

'...The mind is its own place, and in itself can make a Heaven of Hell, a Hell of Heaven...'

John Milton — Paradise Lost

I lose count, somewhere between a Hail and Holy Mary
as my thumb and index bear the imprint of a half rosary.
I cross over the Charles Bridge or, is it the 59th Street one
to Brooklyn, Long Island and beyond,
or is it just an arc of light up on the landing stairway?
If it's not, I tilt my head towards the crucifixion,
the Vltava runs on in to Europe beneath my feet,
to my left, a city of spires pierce domes of hope.
In streets tourists spread out as red imperialists
plundering locals with foreign exchange rates
to buy faith - water fonts and child of Prague's,
religiosity reshapes a cargo hold of Samsonites.
Christendom hangs by front doors, a curiosity
for non believers who believe in, what?
...and blest is the fruit of thy womb Jesus...
I join in again as if skipping without rope
an elbow in the ribs prompts me to my decade:
On Brooklyn Bridge, with hands held out to tickle air
down Broadway and on in to Time Square
sky scrapers seek a heaven in their elasticity of dreams
built by immigrant hands, in search of home.
And in a darkened doorway a Cuban saxophonist sits,
notes come out as ticker tape to whiten hoods and heads,
Dannyboy climbs walls, into bars and on to dash-boards.
Up along Fifth I pick a few crotchety quavers out, take
the mountain side, from glen to glen, on in to St Patrick's:
through the Rose window I see Dean Swift's St. Patrick's
back in Dublin, and there I think of St. Patrick's Asylum
where no amount of Glory bee's might have saved him.
He rocked as Bill Haley had not, the Hail Holy Queen's
would send him in to the middle of next week, to stare
at nothing, something in nothing would stare back at him
shaking the darkness in his day light snow-dome;
flecks of personality a drift — fall, down, down, to ground
(like London Bridge or the Berlin Wall).

46

The liquorice all sorts of a mind assembles on top of d'other
like bodies in a concentration camp, in the productive years.
Prayers and grey matter fertilise earth beneath playing fields.
...*mother of mercy hail our life our sweetness and our hope*...
His days are spent with reeds that sun takes moisture from
bends what is not to be, in under strong sally's, in an up
over weave, baskets galore from a locked wing.
On a clear day along structural steel his footprints echo still,
across Mid-Town, above crowns and clouds, he walks on
in to the nebula of a cosmos he could have had, but for the grace
of his maternal loss adjuster, *as it was in the beginning, is now*...
On Dublin Bay bells keen out or, is it just left of Ellis Island?
Maybe 'tis the belfry in his head that rings in the years aloud.
With the heel of my hand on his forehead, I'd say
he is far from the humidity of cities,
the suspension of bridges, and the opera of sea spray.
Veins marble his temples, waves in a motionless ocean.
I believe in lighthouses, in the kneeling power of prayer,
in the communion of sinners as another glorious mystery,
that hope betrayed is ever green in the waters of memory
and in the life of the world to come, has gone.

Glorious Abacus Mysteries

Do you remember that first communion watch
rapped up in a bidding prayer, caught in beads,
blue beads, Aunt Nan bought in Manger Square?
Midnight with a touch of amethyst she'd say
or was it the navy of a Greek sheep's eye
that hid between her breasts more out of habit.

No less a white *Silvermint* she'd be in the habit
of communing on her tongue after an *Afton*, watch
-ing the match with a ginger snap and an eye
glass. By halftime your wimple is off as beads
of sweat brake out. For tea a collation of say
corned beef and a few soda bread squares.

With your half-crown I buy almond squares
and clove drops, might help you kick the habit.
Chanting twelve times tables as if an office, say.
Lost in sum you top and tail carrots, watch
water orange. You love to take away red beads
from blue, to move wooden circles along the eye

of cat-gut, to figure out complex equations eying
straight forward solutions like St. Peter's Square.
Even playing marbles you'd multiply beads:
click of green spins blue, divides shade's habitat.
In beggar my neighbour, nave of hearts watches
your touch of grace with clubs and spades to say

nothing of poker. At night we'd go to say
Calcutta, to see mud huts with a clear eye.
The host in the sky fills an equinox watch
bisecting darkness in our courtyard square.
A fox nuzzles the hen house like a bad habit
in the light's crack; their eyes are water beads.

On the bed our elbows are triangles, your beads
weave the hulls of our hands, prayers we say
are ships cast into night like an anchor of habit
over sleep's ocean, shipwrecked beyond the eye
of dreams in a myth from some majestic square
rounding a sun dial, winged ones keep watch.

Into gingham you commend a watch of beads
like a turquoise habit of prayer as just say
lavender sails pass through the eye of squares.

In the Family

You lay Aunt Hannah's tablecloth out, sent some eight decades or so
smooth ivory creases from Chicago linen like a district mapped;
Carrickmacross lace in a Lakeshore stitch, crosses imagined gridlines.
Her fine sightedness guides the crooked need of smaller loops through
their rounder selves, threading holes into pattern as a tongue that's lost
its dialect, cadences arranged and rearranged spreading a twang across
air mails and Christmas cards, hung-looping from your chimney breast.
Bone handled knives and forks, the last of the wedding gifts, are put out
with military precision, glinting in sunlight all facing the right way. Start
on the outside and work in said a first cousin once removed, like Yanks
joining forces with the British in the middle east ...*Her eyes they shone
like diamonds you'd think she was Queen of the land*...blades face inward
haw on stainless steel rubs fingerprints out. Burgundy reddens Hannah's
cloth, darkening your valley below Keeper Hill... *and her hair flung over
her shoulder wrapped up in a black velvet band*... Over roast beef and turnip
we'll cross the Atlantic like laces in Jim's boots climbing the Matherclay
to herd Friesians like Black and Tans, as the Land Commission carves notions.
Into parsnips you commend buttered parsley, earthed by a drop of Jameson
makes shadows not seen beyond the haggard as you hang your smalls out:
Jim arcs from hawthorn, heather purples his mind, violet pales indigo.
Shades shade the life from him as one who had a turn. Dusk sets sail —

11

In turn you'll light the pudding left over after Christmas, figs and dates
you've mixed with candid peal, all rum bound, waterproof twine sealed.
Steam will rise as if a Free State beneath a crown. Napoleonic Brandy
flames this fruit-hill as the Sheanafork ablaze; below Tower Hill House
burns dark, as if a Martello alighting Hannah's coastline at Queenstown
as she sets sail for the God of a new world, to the mouth of the Hudson.
...RING, RING...yes the Americans are coming they'll be here by dinner...
Get the Belleek butter-dish and Waterford glass out, got on the Sealink
voyaging east for Holyhead; southward through Shires by the London
train, to look-up those Castle Waller Boland sisters now of the Kings Road.
... no...not the Arklow Pottery bought from them Green Shield Stamps...
those three graces of our North Riding...*London Bridge is falling down...*
teaching English to Chelsea children, like the monasteries dissolution.
*...falling down, my fair lady...*the bells of St. Clements seldom come back
*...oranges and lemons...lemons...*do they know Kickam's Knocknagow?
No not the Royal Dulton got in Cleary's from the two thirty at Lepordstown.
We meet at the Ritz no less, sip Earl Grey, talk of Hannah's husband
shot in the line of duty, lying under the star spangled banner; a half-crown
we tip, disappear into the crowd like race goers at some Irish Sweepstakes
whose place has fallen not long after the starting gun. No stewards' inquiry
nor photo-finish for Hannah who has furlongs to go and off-spring to mind.

Mind you it's all a bit of a cod don't you think, dashing about in our Sunday
best to break bread with Hannah's grandchildren, as seen in Kodak snaps.
Nevertheless, they'll tell us who's on first way out there in Wrigley Fields
and the crowd on their feet going mad, waiting for grown men to strike,
...*what, no Bristol Cream in the trifle, he's been dry a while now so keep*
the pudding out of his vision... yes, Mia Farrow's aunt lives over the way
where that United Irishman, Lord Edward sojourned before he saw dawn
stretching its arms across his last sky. And no doubt we will have to listen
to how great Kennedy was, we've our very own Hockey, as the British say,
to lead us into temptation, so *rise and follow Charlie for a nation once again...*
Your tin church sails from Wales; Rearcross men dovetail its eves, as hands
in prayer, stands in all weathers beyond Flannery's haberdashery come-grocery
and petrol pump, a before-its-time gas station with an Austin Ten on blocks
as Liam becomes Father Austin, ...*we're on the road to God knows where...*
For had you gone, would cars be everywhere, might Maureen O' Sullivan,
or Lucile Ball have known your devotion to the Adelphi screen on Saturdays?
Liberty Hall's your Empire State in this republic, finding its gait in each stride.
Grandfather tic-tocks like a cease fire: windows fog, wicks burn, the roast
stands still, while on the hour young cuckoo patrols the kitchen sink.
In and out of the dining room you go, touch starched napkins along their folds
count butter knobs and melon balls, finger passed-down desert forks,
wondering if you're about to hold the weight of Hannah's history in your hands.

Worlds Apart Together

You sharpen the butt of a pencil, HB I think, cedar-wood
shavings curl like smoke in the woods where Thomas lights sticks,

remembering his boy scout days; that moss grows on the north
of oaks finding south on the palm smoothness of bark.

At Mass Rock outlawed monks celebrated our Lord's word
against Brehon Laws, under the architecture of trees

a cathedral of language lodges in the flying buttresses of leaves,
trunk-naves and the pews of branches, as stain-glass-light tunnels

eaves then and now, a ribbon of sky skirts yew tops, curls
like a tangerine divesting its skin, exposes itself for all the world

to see: flesh, pit and segments as rubber filings drown in ink stains,
dark pools on a school desk mirrors trees billowing a breeze with a birds

-eye view of salmon-king-protea on Table Mountain, where elephant
dassies soak limestone heat, run a westward eye by the Twelve Apostles,

orange-breasted sunbirds, and coastal fynbos stretching south to Hout Bay
as scarlet ibis flame corrugated shanty towns on the road to Plettenberg Bay,

where birds of paradise line ditches, before darkness see-saws dying light
like a key; unlocks chambers dank with musk like frankincense in search

of myrrh. Deep in the depths of Cango Caves Romanesque columns rise
and hang, floor to ceiling: Organ Pipes, Cleopatra's Needle and the Frozen

Waterfall, freeze time as stalactites and stalagmites. Look, see Cape Point
peer into waters where in Sixteen Eighty that Flying Dutchman went down

like roots being put down or the one Thomas digs at with his lead pencil,
teases rhododendron tubers planted by British to attract pheasants and shoot

-ing parties. Funny how his palms hold-open the head of a nail, dead centre,
he doubts if fingering this graphite wound will ease its impression any less.

Hibernia

Nutmeg opened trade routes as the British spread ground troops
all over the John Joe's atlas, before Lourdes or the London Blitz.

His finger follows rivers, bridges and towns not mapped by
the pineapple-crown, where wars will begin, songs will be sung:

from the bless it Magna Carter to the charmin' Trevelyan
from John's New Bible to New Found Land,
from Alice Springs to where they pick Darjeeling Tea

Hail Britannia, Hitler and Holy Queen
Hail our life our sweetness and our hope...

Cucumber triangles, Afternoon Tea at the Carlton-Ritz
scones and clotted cream: *The White Cliffs of Dover,*
going over and over, and Vera Lynn on the Isle of Capri,

Earl Grey sipped from China cups made in England.
Hadrian's Wall the Roman gift of boundary
and the *Walls of Limerick* danced in parish halls, all over

Éire, like coming out of a cold era or the lost city of Pompeii,
with a confidence of a garrison town or the red hand of Ulster
or Michael's hand as he signs *Collins* under The Treaty.

Hail Britannia, Hitler and Holy Queen
Hail our life our sweetness and our hope...

And like London Bridge Big Mick falls down
yer man who shot him will sleep in John-Joe's barn.

In New South Wales echoes of it's a *Long Way To Tipperary*
sound under foot, across oceans, on the beaches, and in Dunkirk.

It could be 1066 or the days of Billy of Orange every July
look at the invisible lines the empire draws,
six orange segments, blood red marbled green.

Hail Britannia, Hitler and Holy Queen.

Letter from the Front

Lately your talk is all tongue and cheek
of how hard it is make ends meet
what with fuel coupons and a ration book

of how a half crown buys nylons and Spam
pawn brokers flourish as the enemy advances.
Silent Night lets both sides climb barricades

acknowledging why three wise men travelled.
Our hands gather, shaping snow into a man
-made thing that bleeds white on Boxing Day.

Second time round, it is more or less the same
black markets and home-guard
on the ground iron out boundaries and air space

before B Fifty-Twos become cocktails, air-fix glue
and Humbrol paint are common place
before Dresden is considered for figurines,

spare arms scatter trenches as mannequins
and so you read the old into the new.
Petals fall as the sun sets in our rose hulls.

Butcher Shop

Your ease with flesh slips palms under skin liking
an ability to steal time out of a Hector Grey tick-tock,

leaves Greenwich Meantime behind the Pacific.
To be specific you tailor the cut of prime rib eye:

the flow of double yellow lines break streets.
On d'telly a priest waves a red-fresh hanky.

In the cold room a makeshift basin hides,
to save face you shave a day's growth.

An apron wipes steel dry.
You wash hands and shut up.

The Failed Bridge

Too hot to sleep and I climb the stair for open air
the flat roof holds July's humidity in its night sky
a blanket with no fire escape from short breaths.

I look out along the Fifty Ninth Street Bridge
towards Queen's, the water tanks are watch towers
as seen from the Belfast train, to keep an eye on things:

on the serge of grass and hedge row,
the movements of cattle across rights of way
and on the ripening of blackberries.

I buy tea with a crown minted in staunch vaults
eager to dig heels into a last foot hold of another country.

A red-blue rain weathers change, salts a belief in
barbed wire over fences. In green fields Union Jacks fly.

And Jack the lad builds ships, bound for storms of eye
-less prayers said with an ease of the linen weave key,

sails nights' ocean on course for star-less victory
where two knots forward takes generations back.

Mist chills darkness as the train pulls in and I think
of Kingstown Pier — no half masts salute sea-spray.

A fog horn rings ripples in across the Hudson
to Angelus bells South East of Scotsman's Bay,
a pale West. Our compass has lost its true North.

Good Friday in September

'Give me your tired, your poor, your huddled masses yearning to breathe free…'
Emma Lazarus — The New Colossus

I bend down, over succulent bushes, to pluck potential jam
blossoms sport a hint of flesh with ripeness just out of reach.
Light loosens green fisted berries blackening tight red knots,
fruit that a fork will squash sun from, sugar draws black out.
Ten half moons finger purple in memory of a blood leach
or stitches taut, fresh from the fall out of New Amsterdam.

East of Wall St. you leg-it in to South. St. Sea Port
an extra in this home movie made, in Afghanistan;
by a tent a Ronson lights a Camel up for Uncle Sam
blue rings waft sands from Long Beach to Kurdistan.
And a swimmer pulls in the tide as an oasis in a kiss,
silver tongued Judas-fish shine mother of pearl skin.

In slow motion you assume the distance of a dream
with sound down, stockbrokers and concrete fall
footsteps lose stride, as clouds rent a sidewalk,
burnt steel flares nostrils with the scent of attack
in God we trust, with a pyramid on a green back
sporting vision as a myopic eye – iris, pupil, look.

You go down to the river and into the river you go
out the mouth of the Hudson tug-boats ferry you, past
Liberty and Ellis, through waves our people took,
currents connect the ins and outs of Hades. Below
Charon collects president's heads, slotted in nook
of oars, rowing usher elect of his touring theatre cast.

I lift my lamp beside the golden door a hand to hoist
white horses, to carry you as sea spray, across oceans
on to main lands, to give life to cacti blossoms
up on this up turned earth, turned over. Into clay
I lay a washed out jam jar full of uprooted poppies.
Blackberries linger around the rim of this globe.

The Weight of the World

Through diminished waters of rippled histories and narrow docks:
tall ships, topsails and gunwales entered the mouth of Alexandra's Basin.

You take the six-fifty from Kingstown to Connolly, past Westland Row
where a banknote vision sinks new foundations into a Viking town below

sea level, like a pin cushion or St. Sebastian, an odd odours of sanctity
rises beneath cobbles, west along Charlotte's Dock for George's Quay.

At the junction of Common and Mayor, dry concrete stretches clouds
fingers an arabesque sky, makes your little Wall Street heaven bound.

And you in a crisp pink shirt with lavender cuffs might cut a dash
towards Bendini & Shaw for pastrami and rye or a shot of Turkish

coffee between selling futures. Half alive before the bell, rung out by
home time, keeping time for the keepers' sake in ten bob note way

as tellers touch Lady Lavery's watermark: the freedom of Nineteen
Sixteen, how pounds, shillings and pence sized the round half-crown.

Dunlop white walls make for Boland's Mill, soft sieved flour freewheels
a sterling light shaft, clouds a magazine blizzard of hand arms, threefold.

By seventy-two corners are knocked off the thrupenny bit, after Christ
in two thousand and two the quid is added to the dead (November list).

Outside the Seven-Eleven awaits another Canary Wharf or Nine Eleven
knowing not the hour nor the day future elegies will be borne. Your main

obsession is weather, if it's too cold for snow. You look from this square
view out the twenty-first floor, in the distance rain is falling somewhere

invisible battlements of the mind, as it was in the beginning, purgatory,
and a breeze within a breeze is your soul seeking its own blue autopsy.

Boatshed at Annaghmakerrig

White pillars hold a red corrugated roof in place, above
a royal blue towel abandoned by skinny-dippers, lies strewn
below July's moon, waits for sun to steal water from light.

I tip-toe through the heart of an algae tractor tyre, wade out
and out, into a murky brown warmth necking my flesh
as six swans glide by to leave a pattern of eight in their wake.

From a table, chairs are pulled back in Gleneagles for the G8.
A horsefly face to face with lake water, glass-like,
as if a passenger looking out from the navy Piccadilly Line.

A lifebuoy moored to a pontoon floats as if a *Polo* Guy
places on his tongue, on the top deck of the No. Thirty
Bus to Tavistock Square, watching his world go by.

From the Underground passengers make their way,
fill the lower deck, bleeding-blood fresh like a memory
of Birmingham, Brighton or Canary Wharf.

Swimming deeper, I hear the flip-flop and plip-plop of fry
silvering shallow waters, illuminates firs
lining the other side, planted by the forestry commission.

Deep in the tunnel at Russell Square bodies are dismembered,
swans make a V in the lake, mirrors the victory
sign of bombers before they're blown to kingdom come.

At Kings Cross Station a flower garden shoots up for the lost.
Faces of the missing look out, pasted to walls as if memory
cards in a prayer book. Reluctantly I backstroke to shore.

Soldiering On

1

With each train of thought you lose the run of yourself
let-on to let go of white-rains haven, a make-believe
avalanche craw-thumping: makes signs crosshatch
and the blessed haves and have-nots seek loadstones.
For deceit snows you under belief-bridges, suspend
-ing a complex notion that joins no two ends
arcs across T joints, brackets loosen your ego's triad
fastens, steadfast and steady as she goes through a self-made
motion reaching discovery's edges — square-curved
liking soap's fragrance in the globe of a palm, perfumery
elect holding scents honesty in the dampness of walls
and washed hands: Pilate and Macbeth back from beyond
unchanged like a coat of arms. Legging it through history
histrionics recalls when flesh hid in soap
its de facto manifesto wipes suds out of European eyes.
Bakelite pens sign treaties blind to what lies between lines
softly as sleep claims names adding weight to All Souls Day
the list lengthens day-light saving hours, foreshortened.
Brightness eclipses Nissen huts for exclamations in masonry
souvenirs shattered-to-smithereens mark a calling card
a lunar arrangement similar to Orion's red-blue star artillery.

And when the field doctor administers relief a cruel salvation
awaits as angels climb trenches to jettison Justice's blindfold
for no bed-side manner breaks out in a wall scaling fashion.
If rimless what ifs had read ophthalmologists alphabets
would distance be greater or nearer thy God to thee, would
you know half of what others knew, arresting Cyclop's vision?
In pocket darkness might fingers thumb a monarch's head
off, rub flesh filings over metal rounds, jingling precision
jangles, marches a goose-step tune, strikes up on demand.
Suddenly iron-rain falls: I think of vinyl static, a diamond
needling seventy-eights, his Master's Voice goes round
and around dizzying paper pit bulls,... *Outside the barricade*
by the corner light... what might have been's are fold
-ing creases in the cracks like lost maps... *give me a rose*
to show how much you care... full are your uniform-words
drifting from Dunkirk... *then will come a love that's new...*
as little hulls fill up with blood 'n guts. And faith less reason
broadcasts: airwaves at sea watermark, horseshoe harbours find
slipways to boatshed doors flung back... *we will create a world*
for two... join forces in the darkness echoing... *Lily Marlene*
as wireless elsewhere's receive sunken ships into neutral zones.

For it is out of stone and bronze, figures will be carved
stood up in town-squares to celebrate the spoils of victory
on rectangular pedestals of raised earth, like proud flesh.
Pigeons shall flock to such crowns whitening a strategy
like a platoon that's lost its regiment: trains will pull out
kit-bags put down, as they learn to pick up where they
left-off. In back gardens empirical apples blossom. Sunday's
sun is short of breath, pinks cream blush, as you cut measured
stems from our rosebush. Into a hall you commend their scent
petals fall to ground, little hulls floored in some botanic myth
looking for Eden through a kitchen window: out past the bay
beyond Biscay and back again, trailing moonlight on a beach
salt-water comes in acute-obtuse angles, islands created by
lovers cars thread impressions of premature driving lessons
ghosted by Bloom waving from afar in search of a local Galilee.
When the skies clear clouds are helmets upturned, not a Zeppelin
in sight but, two barbers poles holding the sky up. If asked
say, we were looking for love, we were, just shooting the breeze.
So we'll go on, out past shorelines tracing Sandymount Strand
souls running over our body of a beach, beyond cockles and
flexed muscles, beyond the ingrained trigonometry of sand.

United States of Mind

for Tom

After my brief setback, I threw myself into my work
relinquished all tall orders from short order chefs
refusing to slice Melba toast or rounds for escargot.
Instead, I curls butter, build pyramids on saucers
in the cold room, till cows would come home; rows
of them glint in florescence as though Weir's window
on Grafton Street; or ball Cantaloupes till juices flow,
all the whilst eyeing strawberries lying bare
beside, kiwi and grapefruits at the same eye level
as anchovies, scallops and pink prawns, awaiting
a Marie Rose blush or to be set alight by a lemon wedge
and a parsley sprig. I think of great Aunt Lilly
on Banna Strand, as she picks periwinkles from shells;
with a pin that held a Cassidy pattern, to a would-be frock.

The Mahony twins are cart-wheeling the afternoon away
what with their handstands, run and jump dives, and back
flip summersaults, as if easy over eggs free-ranging a skillet.
Timmy builds sand scrapers, bridges Brooklyn with fisher nets
the jet stream has offered up. The red bucket and blue spade
his Dad bought at the petrol-pump-shop, do most heavy work.
The O'Reilly girls play beach ball (the one his Da didn't buy)
American style, as seen on the Brady Bunch last Friday week.
A pink lucky bag's crêpe paper is opened back by young Emily
with such care, it might well be her eternity ring from Tiffany's
that Timmy will buy her, having tied the knot with his twin, Jack.
She will bear another set of Mahony kids, east of Hudson Bay
where these brothers will continue to draw and redesign this city
and its skyline, in the face of back handers on the road to Teach Bawn.

A spinning top and an orange gob-stopper is all Emily gets for now.
By Tree-Top Rock Mr. Murphy is sinking a tin of Guinness Light.
For one who's full of hot air, he sure can blow his lye-low up, ready
to sail for Byzantium, having staked out a canvas windless boundary
with a blocker. With his hanky he makes four-corners of the globe
cover his bald patch, sunburn light reads the map of his catarrh;
a summer flu got pumping gas into Hayes refrigeration unit. Down
he settles to study the form, read the funnies and Nineteen Eighty Four.
On their knees the Buckley boys are digging out the Hover Dam.
You'd swear they were the ice brigade or high scalars scaling the rock
face, throwing muscle power behind movement, to divert the Colorado.
Blue and red milk bottle tops define their Arizona State line, razor
shells are the Art deco statues holding sway as if Corinthian columns:
driftwood, bleached granite, barnacles and orange periwinkles decorate.

From behind marram grass Joe Gleason is held up, watches Ragtown
and Vegas, makes a telescope of De Velara's Irish Press. Smoke
signals rise from Mrs Flannery; blue *Major* rings ascend as if Christ on
Easter Sunday, or a volley of shots piercing a band of cloud over the GPO.
Between bites of chicken sandwiches left after the dinner, a pack of Tayto
and what with her other half's ear to the Match, she talks to the widow Ryan,
(of the bishop and d'nighty, as aired on Gay Byrne's Late Late television
show). Boy how they bear red Indians stripes for cowboy Joe on his sand
dune; its good sniper training for when he sells his Irishness for a Morrison,
does a stint in Iraq as a storm trooper, while his school pal joins The Black
Watch. Together they will fight for a better world, quash al-Qa'ida, find new
routes through the oil fields of Afghanistan, to help our economies of scale.
They'll see the FTSE and the Dow battle it out in financial graphs on CNN,
the FT and the Wall St. Journal, watch euro gain ground against the dollar,

balance of power struggles muscle. For now Elvis Costello's *Oliver's Army*
plays across the beach on Mrs Buckley's transistor radio, spreads like a rumour —
it's British you know, gets the world wide service, *Oliver's Army is here to stay*
*… and I would rather be anywhere else than here today…*Out of low waves
the O'Reilly girls come, pearls in oyster shells, dressed for wading heavy snow
-drifts: in their long-john togs, frilly-skirts and yellow bathing hats, you'd think
Alaska beckons. Blather wrack Jane holds, as if fishing a blowhole. Young Jack
lets his paper Titanic sail from his palms, out Belfast Lough; stops at Queenstown
and Bartholdi's Liberty, into the mouth of the Hudson before icebergs and breakers.
Club Milks Mrs Buckley hands out, to all in sundry within arms length of her life
as she saves Gary Glitter's photograph, hid under the six bars, for her own kids
not knowing what his own fondness for children would hold… *suffer little children*
to come onto thee for theirs is the kingdom of the world…or that one of the Jackson
Five would become whiter than coke; sugar-drunk on picnic tea and fizzy drinks.

Heinz sandwich spread holds Mother's Pride in place in Attracta Lyon's pink Tupperware box, before that she'd be at doors, with her rouge lips mouthing, *Avon Calling...calling...*now its all plastic coloured evenings, airtight sales, non return -able parties in living rooms the length and breath of the country, with her Texaco map on kitchen tables, from Fair Head to Carnsore Point. Outside Mountmellick Kerrygold smudges appear to circle, ripple-like; as if a stone thrown into water. Last summer's crab apples make their way as jelly across roads in Drumshambo while mother's marmalade peel that was not strained through muslin finds itself skulking about unmarked white clusters, ambering strongly around Portadown, down the right of way near where four brothers were shot for their real belief. So, what colour is betrayal, can you see it on the face of the self-effacing clergy who spit brimstone and hellfire, from their rhetorical pulpits, bullet-like, purpling body and blood and the soul of our saviour who sanctifies our needs, need I say more, anon. Matilda Madigan is at that blasted hula-hoop dance with an orange

swim ring, she thinks she's a vision from Hawaii-Five-O, waiting for Jack to say **book him Danno**. Meanwhile, young Fossetts, are spread-eagle, like the Golden Gate Bridge, arm to shoulder, Titian ringlets touching finger-knuckles and backs of hands. Sun warms their solar plexus, imagining Alcatraz in the distance, for they have read Papillon. Butter-flying through water, strokes into waves like thread -ing a needle, Sheila arcs as if swimming the final seconds of the LA Olympics. With Bobbie's clove-strip straw in his Fanta, he snorkels...off the Gulf of Mexico, to the Orange State, south of Tampa and Sarasota to draw breath at Longboat Key. John and Mabel Ringling's Cà d'Zan sports Michangelo's David in their garden a circus animal's desertion, history galore of fire eating dogs and conjoined twins. This Venetian Palace, its indigo slabs walk into the Gulf. Sheila's right hand touches four deep purpling rings of a see-through jellyfish as if the corners of the earth. Finals of the seaweed hurdles are taking place. The Flannery kids think they're Pony Express running Confederate flags up 'n down the beach, competing with donkey

rides on Banna Strand, clip-clopping wet sand, to trace a shore for One Pound-Fifty. No silks, nor odds on for runners and riders in their make-believe Kentucky Derby. Out, beyond kids doing doggie paddles and belly flops, beyond pink water wings and swimming rings, a snorkel is a submarine eye, bringing Roger Casement ashore and the weight of history to shuck his diaries; as if a square Jacobs biscuit tin on a high up shelf, full of Lady Lavery Pound notes, rolled tight as hazelnuts, ready to be prized — Oh and but what prizes to be won, on d'Irish Hospitals Sweepstakes Draw, and the secret of how to gamble, *if you're not in you can't win,* prohibited under our Charities Act. With a ring at the door of a Friday, our postman would hand over a green bag, for a signature. We'd break the seal. Empty its inside out on our kitchen table, rice paper envelopes flow, red 'n blue trimmed as if Niagara's Horseshoe Falls with air-mail wings from: Nebraska, New Orleans, Detroit, Missouri, Pennsylvania, both sides of the Oregon and Santa Fe Trails towards Mayor Daly's Lake Michigan. From... *the Blue Ridge Mountains of Virginia...to the Black Hills of Dakota...*

from ...*the trail of the lonesome pine*... to Yogi Bear's, Yellow Stone National Park
from the Delta of the Mississippi to where the Yukon flows right through Holy Cross
from the Mormon to the Jew, the southern Baptists to the white hooded Ku Klux Klan
from Key Stone Cops to *Top Cat*, all piled pyre high as if the Silver Mines of Tipperary
or the Gold Rush, each buried under a darkness of another; our hands are light-shafts,
tunnelling hope, to finger immigrants money, the Bill of Rights and the Rights of Man
above the apron where we eat our meals and say the Joyful Mysteries of our rosary.
As an official piggy in de-middle we'd send these letters with president's heads on
to our Sweepstakes Headquarters at Ballsbridge, just before the bridge, Collins often
crossed; and the Ringsend one, before the Star of the Sea church or gun running stuff.
In the name of God, would you credit that, Tom Ahearn is marking sand with a stick,
you'd swear he and his shadow selves were young Mason and Dixon. ...*I have taken*
leave of my chicken farm in Idaho, his namesake wrote to my Grandmother in Foilduff,
I'm in New York, working my passage, be sure to have a goose ready for my Christmas Holiday.

War breaks. Great Uncle Tom disappears, without trace; his line of the family,
rubbed out as though master Tom's beach cartography, vanishes with the moon,
its phases, and the push-pull of dark tides. Although, his brother did go to Montana,
Butte I think, or was it Leadville, along with all those from Beara, in West Cork.
From the promenade a row of white whipped cones approach, as if Mount McKinley
peeks, fresh from Willie's ice cream van. His child-magnet-musical-drone, drowns
the Count's Italian aria's, on his mother's short-wave radio, snug beside Cadbury
flakes, above her red Formica top, where he cuts wafers from the block; uses Daddy's
butchering knife, for the sharp edges. Raspberry ripple runs down little white paws
as a kid licks Willie's curves, skips into a disabled parking spot. *God but I never saw*
him, what with the sun and all, the driver says. The blue-white light of the nee-naw
takes the hit child to St. Michael's Private, where sunburnt parents keep vigil, pray
to the God of Ice Cream Cones, not to take away the sins of the world with Terry's
young life. Blinded by the light he was, like Saul on the road to Damascus, so he was.

Using the bay as a sundial, it makes its way around the arc of tides, throws shadows
as Mrs Flannery's sponge buns can-cover her interior oven-light, making for its roof.
And the roof of mouths, use tongue-tips to free aniseed from her seminal cake. Pink
and beige draught-Battenberg-squares, duck-egg yellow rapped, with fresh marzipan
she rolls of a Sunday, on a marble work-top, came from that old hotel they once had.
She slices Madeira as deftly as the Mahony's Frisbee cuts the sky blue, bleeds navy
white, like sugar lumps widow Ryan drops into her Wedgwood cup of fine Ceylon
tea. God you'd swear she's a WASP holding court, as though at a Boston Tea Party.
Would you credit that, our tartan rug from the Highlands done up like a wigwam,
long handled spades support. We eat shortbread, play Navajo and Apache, television
style, having learned our lines on last week's *Virginia*. Trumpeting shells, its theme
tune heralds a new wave of Tonto and Silver, Rodgers and Champion, horsing about
how the West was won, or more to the point, lost. In the colonisation of a colony,
shades of our empire's hand at bay: diminishes reservations and carved tomahawk

faces, rain-dances, moccasin, the use of feathers and the great wilder-beast-bison.
For heaven's sake, would you look at the state of young Missus Florence Andrews.
Eyes done up like a Macy's mannequin, hair sleeked back with the sea, salt holds
it just so; god, how heads turn as she carries herself from the surf as if Ursula, yet
there's a fair sense of nightingale about her. At least that's what Mr Mahony thinks
of a Wednesday, as they make solar energy catch the dying light in their Barclay
Square of make-believe, three years this Ash. It was after pancakes, before Lent's
purpling weeks, Grace arrived, two years this Shrove. Florence's let-on other half
was lost at sea, so he was. So here's the think. Mrs Mahony keeps their kid's father
from his tea; to vent Florence's radiators, or check her wiring, what with no man
in her house. Mrs Mahony never blows a fuse or figures he's saying the Our Father
with Grace after reading Sleeping Beauty. Two weeks in far off Ballybunnion has
Trish Boland looking like an African Queen. She French polishes her lithe calves
with Johnson's baby oil for a deeper shade of Brazil nut or, mahogany like the tripod

she runs her palms over, before the skin doctor examines her sun damaged liver spots.
In Farrell's bar, over pints and packets of peanuts they still talk of her tan, in the wake
of her anniversary. Laid out in an American quilt, so she was; a square for every state.
Think of all that dam calamine lotion she'd pour on herself, wasn't worth a curse; and
so and so from up the road, and your one from down the way and what do-you-ma-cal
him from over the street, all basked under the same sun, and not a bother nor a blotch
There're off again, Mrs Flannery and the widow Ryan; shots of *Wild Turkey* splashed
with *Canada Dry* helps the afternoon pass; her husband listens for results of his Yankee
the bookmaker took off his hands, he twiddles the dial, all fingers and thumbs. Tunes i
...*the Indians send signal from the rocks above the pass*...remember Squeeze... *cowboys
take position in the bushes and the grass*... *Cool for Cats*...take care fear'n you would
spill that ginger-ale, we need it to watch *Lassie*. Clouds gather. Darkness descends
as if the hand of d'Lord maybe at bay, it's real end of the world stuff. And like a count
occupied, there's a flurry to collect their belongings, as if collecting sins for confession.

Believe you me there's, no accounting for taste, Mr Murphy rescues a Black Forest,
soaked to the skin, a sure sign that he's off his trolley, ling-lang-longing a long.
When rain falls the O'Reilly girls and Mahony boys cover up with coloured towels,
as if four blanket states; piggy-banking sand dollars in empty urchin shells like pension
funds, letting-on to sleep...perchance to dream... time still and the fuchsia of their lives
blossoms before them in their American dream. *Peek-a-boo...Come on, for the love of God
or we'll not be home for The Thunder Birds or Scooby Doo? Not to mention The Magic Round
About,* ... into cars we pile, ready to hit the road; barely making out the man in the moo
its corona or the celestial heavens that we touch, with our fingertips out the back windov
tracing our motion against the Jovian satellites, helping us find our longitude at sea.
The Mahony's, O'Reilly's and me, we are the Famous Five, but will we be? ...*show me
the way to go home,* will we find a ...*place where there's no trouble?*,... *I'm tired and
I want to go to bed...* will we be ourselves with ourselves? ...*I had a little drink about
an hour ago, and its gone right to my head...*Will we find somewhere over the rainbow?